I0171341

"The wound is the place where the light enters you"
-Rumi

Daughter of Babylon

MY TURN

I don't have love poems for you
No long kisses
Stars in their eyes

I have cracking thunder and swift tides
I have spiky thorns and bitter words swallowed

No lovey dovey
No pinks and lavenders

This is cloudy gray
Midnight black
It's evergreen

I've got seeds watered by salty tears
And rivers dug up by searching hands
Valleys I stomped out with my pen

But there's no Adam and Eve
No Vishnu and Shiva

This is Medusa in the cave
Cleopatra after the snake bite
Theodora on the throne
Jezebel with a pen

This is Joan at the stake
Virginia in the lake
Harriet with the musket
Juliet when she rises from the dead and steps over Romeo's body
This is Shakespeare's Sister
This is Pocahontas slitting those colonizers throats

This is not a love poem.

THE QUIET ONE

They want me to speak
They want me to say something

I wonder if they'd be startled if I screamed in their faces
Like a banshee screaming into the night

Well you wanted me to say something.

There it is.

CAT AND MOUSE

I used to think that great people
Had great sorrow
And that's what made them great

So I went around looking for pain
I chased it down
Thought it would give me
Steel wings.

But instead
I was swallowed
I played with fire and got burned
3rd degree.

I had to retreat
Lick my wounds.

But the flames still looks nice from afar.

SWEPT AWAY

I have a love-hate relationship with rainy days.
On one hand they're pretty
Almost ethereal
When you're inside

But when you're caught in it
Rain pounding
Wind whipping

You feel as if you
Could get swept up and away
You feel your fragility
Mother nature's fierce strength.

You realize you are
A blimp in time
Easily blown away

But this rain is forever.

OPENING SCENE

For whatever reason I thought I could catch it.
So there I was running in pouring rain.
The type of rain that pounds into the ground
That stings.

I thought if I run a little faster I'll catch it,
I'll be there, all this will be worth it.

I was a few feet away from the entrance,
The clock had just turned and the wind
Had a personal vendetta against me,
Because every step I took
It pushed back.

Got in and I was soaked head to toe.
My blue jeans where
Soaked through
And I watched the tail of the
Train speed off.

I didn't quite feel the cold until I saw that train leave
Didn't realize how soaked I was

Cold, alone, and
There it goes.

NAIVETY

Maybe I'm naïve
That's why I get hurt so easily.

But I want to see light
And believe
In light.

Some writers go on and on about the darkness,
How agony is the only constant.
but what is pain without joy?

and pain isn't forever
I want to see the beauty in the day.

I'm done
Writing my sob story.

Okay maybe
Not done

But there is more than pain

I know that

It's about
the only thing
I know.

EXHALE

There are moments of clarity
Where everything is
Okay

Nothing has changed
My situation is the same

But for a brief moment
I breathe in
And exhale
And I'm Okay
And I feel free

I feel alive
I feel present
Not in a disillusioned trance
Not dreamlike

But I can feel the wind
On my face
And I feel good
Without anything
Changing
Like a film has been lifted from my eyes
And everything is lighter
Easier.

DORIAN GRAY

Young
Youth
The golden years
The best days of your life

Bullshit
Bullshit

All I am is confused
I have no clue
Who I am
Or what I want
Or where I'm going

I'm scared and
All you say is

"These are your best days"
I guess?
"It's all downhill from here"

As if that isn't the most depressing shit I've ever heard
I might as well jump off a cliff now

I refuse for <u>this</u> to be the peak of my life

NO.
Nope.
Not happening.

My life at 45 will be infinitely better
Than now
Even if I have to make it happen
Out of spite.

DRAMA QUEEN

I didn't think I'd be the person who needs coffee every morning
But when I woke up and my favorite
Travel mug was gone
I almost jumped off a (small) cliff.

It's all I could think of all morning
When I was freezing, cold, waiting for the train
I thought
"This would be a great time to take a sip of coffee".

You might be thinking
Why not get a different mug?
But there was no different mug

All the other mugs couldn't hang with me
My mug was resilient

It could get dropped
Get knocked over
And still be good

Hours later
Still warm

But no
The stars were not aligned
For me today
My mug was gone.

A LITTLE HARSH

The aesthetic of "the greats"
Is appealing

The cigarettes
The bottles of liquor
As they type away at the typewriter

The stories of love
War
Poverty on the streets
The fear, the unrest

They managed through it all
To write a good poem

They sat at their typewriters
And viewed the world

Wrote what they saw
What they thought
Like those eyes in Gatsby

But that liquor chewed out their livers
And those cigarettes burned their lungs
And those white men passed away thinking

Well, I don't know, I can't assume what they thought

But in the end we read their work
And still consider them great

But by what standard?

The aesthetic is great and they had something to say
But it's not worth romanticizing

Their time passes and their stories
Lie in those graves with them.

MORE THAN ENOUGH

I don't have epic love stories
Or tragic war tails
I don't have campfire wisdom or insight
I don't have stories of drunken anger or scandalous romance
Maybe I don't have the material that "the greats" had
But I have black girl sorrows
And that's gonna have to be enough.

RESSURECTION

It amazes me
That I can break one night
And put myself back together
By morning.

SITTING ON THE EDGE

Everyone's supposed to pick their struggles
Right?

We all feel pain and suffering
You just have to find a purpose
For that suffering

And what if I don't know
My purpose?

I've reached a threshold
A point of wanting to throw
It all away

But I'm afraid
Afraid I'm wrong
Afraid I'll be out there
With no safety net

If I risk everything
And throw it away

What will it be for?
That, I at least need to know

Before I risk everything
I have to know
I need to know what I want.

OVERFLOWING GLASS

What's worth suffering for?

I want to be ok.
I want to be OK.

I know I can't avoid pain
But I want to

Is that a bad thing?

My brain is overwhelmed about what?
Why am I so confused?
Maybe because I'm trying to find all the answers
When there are none.

THEY PROBABLY DO

I wonder
If people who write self-help books
Factor in chemical imbalances?

THREE DAY WEEKEND IN BABYLON

I want to indulge in the maladaptive
Just for a moment

Dip my toe in the pond and
Let my mind swim around
Unburdened by right or wrong

To just feel
For a second
Even when I know it's bad

And "bad", a word
What does it mean?
Who decides?
And in what context?

Do you ever want to do something?
Something you shouldn't?
Just to see how it feels

I think we all do sometimes
But common sense stops us
But reality checks us.

DRINK UP BUTTERCUP

Sadness sinks in like a breeze
Felt through the trees
Flows into my lungs

A deep breath
A chilling antidote
My brain has grown accustomed to it
Craves it even

I wean myself off
Only to find it hidden in my water

Lying dormant at the bottom
Of my cup
Like a parasite slipping down
With each gulp.

DECISIONS DECISIONS

There are things that I want
And I'm unsure if this moment is one of them.

If I ran away
Where would I go?

An escape
Is what I crave

But maybe instead of running
I need to stay

Running without a plan
Is careless

Where are you running to?
What are you running from?

I'm stuck in a pinwheel
A carousel

Stuck.

If I stop running
Where does that leave me?

I want answers to questions
No one can answer

Things that no one can give me

And it's a nightmare.

DEMONS PERSONIFIED

To be stuck
To have one's feet in cement
And the only one who can see it
Is you

This is the part where I'm supposed to
Write something inspiring

Where I tell you
to break the cement

but this isn't that poem
this is the last skip
that a stone makes
before sinking into the pond.

RUMPELSTILTSKIN

I'm hoping to spin gold
Out of wool

To turn my pain
Into triumph

It's a cliché
But one that I cling to.

Because if pain doesn't serve a lesson
If there is nothing to gain from this moment
From the next
What's the point?

SPYGLASS

At the bottom of my glass
Is a letter.
One that I can't make out.

I drink a little more
And peer into the glass
Like an explorer looking
Into a telescope

Still fuzzy
I drink a little more

The same amount
Sits in the cup

Still blurry
I look again
To find the letter gone
Swallowed.

CRACKED CHALKBOARDS

Who gets to make the interpretation?
Is an important question.

Why is the authors opinion not put into perspective?
Why they wrote what they wrote?

Who's writing is this for?
Who's the audience?
Who gets to decide?

If I write that the audience is X
If I say in an interview that I had this in mind

Do my words fall flat?

Is your scholarly opinion,
Your answers more important than
My intentions?

So you're going to say
What I meant?

So you know what I was thinking?

Despite some scholarly opinion
Poetry, art, is tied to the artist
Like a root to a branch

If I say this is what I meant
I said what I said

The artist, the background
It's important.
It matters.

By detaching the work from the artist
You do not gain greater insight

Everything I write might not be
About me
But it is me
Because I wrote it.

Think about that
Do a lecture on it
Take out your pen and
Analyze it.

YEAH, I SAID IT (SCHOOL DAZE ANGER)

There's a clear divide from inside the building
And outside.

The people inside sit around conference tables
They sit behind desks
They stand in front of the room

They present, they discuss
In a matter of minutes
They find the "answers"

They find "answers" to
Imaginary questions for what purpose?
And what is gained?

There's something laced in this water
The water fountains don't taste right

So that person up there in the front
Knows all the answers
And what if I disagree?
What does that get me?

Does having a degree make you an expert?
Does it make you undebatable?

Am I supposed to feel stupider?
In your presence?
Are your words supposed to mean more than mine?
Because you have a method?
Because you have a scholarly perspective?

MAYBE YOU DON'T HAVE ANY: ME TOO

No one has it all figured out

People simply have more information
Or have done more

There's more information
But that doesn't mean they "know"

There are facts and then
There are unknowns

There are more unknowns
than facts

All anyone can do is guess
So remember that

Just because they said they have all the answers
Doesn't mean those answers are right

Or undebatable
Or written in stone

It means that is what <u>they</u> know
To be true
Those are the answers <u>they</u> found

What are your answers?

DEAR AUTHOR

People with pens
Make markings
They break things down
They ask questions like "what's the voice"
"who's the audience"

they say
"this what they meant
this is who they are talking about"

guesswork
writing with black pen
on black paper
in the dead of night

it's not fruitless
but what do you gain?
but your own satisfaction of being right

of course they meant something

but did they mean that
I'm not sure
Maybe we should ask them.

PICKING LOCKS AND KICKING DOWN WALLS

I'm a little ticked off
Lava seeping from my pen
It's hard to pinpoint

Somethings not sitting right
In my brain.
A round peg trying to be jammed
into a square hole.

I had to get away
From the noise
Because every sound
Was a cymbal crashing in my ear.

It has something to do with
Being told what to think
Something about squares
Lots of squares

Stale toast
Something bitter and bland

It's stiff, no movement
Not free flowing

It feels final, absolute
And I don't like it.

I can't quite put my
Finger on it

But it felt like being caught in a net
With a school of fish, I don't belong to.

GOLDILOCKS

Somethings are funny
In that not funny way

It's funny how you can say
In so many words what I just said but
Your words are profound
And mine are chicken meal

It's funny how when I say it
You don't hear me but then you
Repeat me like a tape recorder

I create, you get credit
That's how it works
In your world
Mine is a little different
My sound is hollow
Through your vocal cords
Flat, off pitch.

ONE TICKET TO MENTAL BREAKDOWN PLEASE

I couldn't stop crying on the train
In the corner
I sniffled and whipped away tears quickly
People glanced at me then glanced away
Never said anything
Got on and then got off

I cried in the car on the way home
my vision blurred
I cried walking to the door
Cried while I untied my boots

And then something took over me
more than just crying
My sobs turned into wales
I was cutting through water
I was crashing against the waves
I was tethered to a rock dragging me down

I was choking
Gagging on my own tears
Wave after wave after wave.

FUN HOUSE STROLL

I'm scared
Scared that I won't live up to my own expectations
Scared that another year will go by and I'll have nothing to show
for it
Scared that I'll regret my past decisions
Scared that I'm not doing enough
Scared that I'm missing out on what life's really supposed to feel
like

I'm just so afraid
I don't want to fail and fall flat on my face
But I've got to
I've got to try
But right now I'm just scared.

I HAVE TO START SOMEWHERE: THIS LOOKS GOOD

I'm tired of everyone's expectations and opinions
They always have something to say

This is <u>my</u> life
Me
I

And I've got to be the one to make my decisions

I'm hitting the mute button
This isn't your story
It's mine

I've got to learn my own lessons
Make my own mistakes

Me and only me.

I CAN SHOW YOU THE WORLD

One day I'll paint the world I see with this pen

It'll be fairly lights dancing in the moonlight
It'll be rose petals floating in the air
Stars that shine and light up the midnight sky
Water sweet like honey
Trees stretched to the sky

It'll be whimsical caught in a whirlwind of wonder
And I'll be there
The woman in the gown stretched out behind me

Floating on air
I'll do the waltz in the clouds and I'll sing
To the birds and they'll sing back
Lovely melodies of enchanted gardens and water nymphs

With a stroke of my pen I'll paint the sky, shift the mountains,
And dot my i.

CARNIVAL RIDES AND POPCORN

Sometimes my demons
Are
Tap
Tap
Tap dancing
On my temples

Just to get under my skin
They know just the right things to do
But I won't let them win

And I'm jumping through hoops
Hula hooping
While doing a balancing act

One pin, two pin, three
All hovering in the air
Screaming
"catch me"

and I'm trying alright
my hearts pounding alright
and as they begin to descend
and my veins are popping from concentrating

and tap
there goes pin #1

tap tap

pin #2
down down
slips through my fingers

tap tap tap

pin #3
oh pin #3
so close
almost caught it but
fumbled at the last minute

so all that's left
are these tap dancing demons
and my hula-hoop.

PLANTING INSTEAD OF RIPPING UP ROOTS

This isn't pseudo positivity
Or pretending I never made mistakes

It's not being self-deprecating
It's acknowledging that I messed up
That I can take responsibility and learn
and grow
That's all I can do

And then maybe
I can begin to heal
Instead of picking at myself.

YOU'VE GOT A NICE SMILE

I know I write a lot of sad poems

A lot of battling and demons
But I'm grateful for the light that's in my life.

I have a good life
Despite how it seems on these pages
And forever I'm appreciative of all those that make my day a little
brighter

And I'm hopeful
For a future that's filled with
More laughter
More hugs
More light.

A REMINDER ON WHAT YOU ALREADY KNOW

You never know how someone feels until they tell you

We read into body language
Glances
But we get it wrong

We project
See with bias
Filters
So be careful
About your assumptions.

TAKE IT FROM ME

I've learned
Over time
That very few things matter more
Than your sanity

Protect it
The rest of it can wait
The rest of it is irrelevant

If you lose yourself
And your mind
In the process

What is the point?

EASIER WRITTEN THEN DONE

When you look fear in the face
And take a step through it
You realize that fear is only
A mirage

And that you have the power
To see beyond it
 by drinking from your fountain of strength

looking fear in the face isn't not being afraid
it's stepping through your fear
and doing it anyway.

WILD CARD

There's a turning point
When you realize that playing by other people's rules
Doesn't work

You have to find your own way
To live this life
And it doesn't have to make sense to everyone else

Define success for yourself
Step back and think about it all
All the preconceived notions of what you should be doing
And start thinking about what you can do

You can do so much more than what others can imagine for you.

THEY SAY "WHAT DOESN'T KILL YOU MAKES YOU STRONGER": BULLSHIT

I've seen first hand
Life crumble around someone
I've also seen the foundation strengthen under their feet
As they got back up

But Tearing ourselves down is easy
Building ourselves up is difficult

Trauma doesn't make you stronger
You do that

It's a choice.

DANGEROUS JENGA

People don't realize that
Trauma can build on itself.

Like a tower of dominos
Each incident adding to the height
It only takes one.

One shaky placement
For it all to come crashing in around you

Something to an outsider
Might seem like an isolated incident
But I know how high my tower is
So forgive me
If I'm cautious of who I play games with.

FISH CAUGHT IN A NET

I don't want to feel stuck
Caught in a never-ending loop

I'm afraid I'll be in the same spot for too long

Despite my life changing all the time
It's easy to feel stuck sometimes

I'm trying to figure out what's bothering me
What's going on in my mind?

EARLY LIFE CRISIS

I don't have the energy to play the
Coulda, shoulda, woulda, game anymore

I could've made different choices
Maybe they would've been better
But those choices
Are gone
Floated away by the wind
As I walked down another path
And even if that path
Led me to fall and skin my knees
There's no turning back

Wondering and wishing has taken up too much energy
And too much time

I just want to
Live

Not survive
Not wonder
But live

Without those mistakes
Without that fall
I wouldn't have learned my lessons.

MY SLICE OF NARNIA

Looking for yourselves in someone else's eyes
is a mistake

we get caught up in the whim of it all
the whisking away
the floating on air
the whispers swept up in the wind

we paint long strokes of magenta and orange
on the blue sky with our eyes

we float in the clouds
with birds chirping in our ear

but we forget the crashing waves against the rocks
the sun that stings a little too much

I only want to see the magic and sparkle
I want to cast spells and dance under the moon

But we've both got stars in our eyes and no space ship
Dreams of grandeur
And no stairway to heaven

I'm no angel and you're no knight
You can't fight for me

I'm the princess in this fairytale
And the dragon

We've gotten so caught up in the myth of it all we forgot reality.

I SAID WHAT I SAID

I made a promise to myself
That I would never immortalize a man on these pages.

No man deserves to live forever on MY pages.
No man deserves the stroke of my pen.

IN NEED OF A LOCKSMITH

One week, Two week, Three
This month, that month
This job, that job

The box that society has put me in
I've found the key

I'm tired of counting the days
Making the tally marks
Passing the time

Clock in clock out
This command that command

I'm over it
I'm over it all

I'm gonna have to rewrite the roles
The rules
Change my formula

It's time to pass this bar
Ace this test
Because I'm tired of listening to other people's lectures

You can't give me advice on what you don't know
To many people that don't know
Want to comment.
To many boxed people.

WHERE'S THE FINISH LINE?

I want things to be simple
Is it bad that I want things to be easy?

Negative feelings and failure are a part of life
But when is it too much?

Where's the threshold?
Where negative feelings and adversity start to consume you?

My mind is my own worst enemy
My own thoughts are racing each other against an imaginary clock

Tick tock
I just want to turn off this track.

TURTLE AND THE HARE

I have to challenge my notions of what I think is OK

I keep getting caught up in the steps
I need to do,
This by this time or what?

What happens if I move a little slower?
But enjoy the ride more?

NINA SIMONE DREAMS

We all have whimsical dreams
And mine is no fear
No pain
An unrealistic life of simplicity and ease

A life where my problems aren't existential
But simple
And easy to solve

Everything these days seems too complicated
So many steps
So many expectations
So little time

I think I don't want to do this, but I have to
Who says so?
What will I lose?
What will I gain?
When will I stop worrying?

I'm trying to live up to an expectation
An expectation that I'm not sure exists outside of a myth

Whose values am I judging myself against?

THE REVOLUTION WILL NOT BE TELEVISED

We've become engrossed in each other's lives
Always plugged in
The opulence, the luxury
It's kings and queens on every screen
Everyone wants to look like that
Live like that

The American Dream
A Dream
Festering and blistering in the hot sun
Rotting in our stomachs
Because we swallowed it like a happy pill

And we chase like a hamster in a wheel

I want it
You want it
But is it worth getting?
Is it even there?
Or is it a ghost
A phantom on the wind of old white mans dream.
Whose Dream?

I don't remember
Ever wanting it until it was presented to me
on a silver platter with a newspaper and glass of water.

WINGS STAPLED TO MY BACK

Songbirds and a wooden table looking out a window

I inhale, I exhale, I listen

The day starts when the sun rises and
Ends when the moon rises
Stargazing is my favorite pass time

Simplicity
Is all I want
But I'm stuck in a labyrinth
Everything is fast and complex

It's this, that
Tit for tat
Everyone's go, go, go

We've got lives to work away
We've got money to make
That's what we've got
We've got more
More than we know what to do with
And some days I'm content with that

And some days I'm drowning in it
And it's not that
I want less

I want more of something different
Something that isn't this.

FINE PRINT: KINGS AND QUEENS IN THEIR OWN MINDS

Everything comes with Terms and Conditions now

Gatekeeping in their big silver suits standing guard
Only the "worthy" get to enter

Get to sit at the round table

Discussing what the people want
What should we give them?
What crumbs should we let trickle off our plates?

And there's not a single commoner at that table
And the reality is
They're not even discussing us
They're discussing themselves

Power is a tricky thing

It's the biggest illusion we play into
We are quick to give it away
To assume someone else has it
To assume that we don't.

SELF FULFILLING PROPHECY

maybe I don't know what I'm talking about
maybe I have nothing new or interesting to say

but I'm here.
and I choose this.

ARCHAEOLOGIST OF THE SOUL

I thought
I was writing my future with these pages.

I realized
I'm remembering my past.

I'm unearthing a memory of
Who I am.

A person I forgot
and filled in the blanks with other people.

GREAT GRANDPA'S SCARS

Do you ever feel a ripple of pain?
that you don't know where it came from?

maybe it
clawed its way out of the cold earth
grasping at the living air
buried with unmarked graves

maybe it drips like a spigot
funneled up through shattered bones
lying at the bottom of the abyss

maybe it dangles like ripe fruit
cut down with a blade
further sinking into your subconscious
until it drops from your eyes

maybe?

YOU ARE HERE

I know how to feel pain
I know what it looks like
I can spot it out in a crowd
I know how to swallow it
toss it around

but I don't know how to feel the rest of it
and that's where the question is

is pain a given?
dissolved into the water I drink?

Is happiness a destination
they sell you in pamphlets?

we've got destinations, but no answers

no anything else
and I'm tired of that

I'm tired of it.

A FOUR LETTER WORD

the stuff of legend
and poetry's gassoline
every writer tries to
capture it on the page
seal it in a glass jar
write it in so many words

it's everywhere you turn
being sold to you
the topic of gossip
the meaning of life

a picturesque
illusion
sawn together with
images and words
spanning from centuries

it's been
prepacked and rewrapped
people spend their whole lives
looking for a mirage

instead of seeing the magic
that breathes in the wind
that lives in the laugh
that swims in our body heat

don't chase that picture
don't try to recreate
the image in your head
live now
and act

because love is action

its action mixed with compassion
and its work
not illusion

all that other stuff is dopamine.

BULL HORN LUNGS

silence is like an illness
it can be passed down
from generation to generation

it can be contracted by hanging out
with the wrong people

it can be contagious
as you watch everyone around you
get sick as well

and you don't even realize it

it's silence
slipping in without you noticing
invisible

but you can feel it's grasp on you
like a weight on your chest

like something caught in your
throat

you live with it so long
you get used to it

you forget what it was like to breathe
without discomfort
you forget what it was like to speak
with your full voice

and so it takes its hold

this is your reminder
that you can breathe deeper

speak louder

remember your voice

and purge the silence.

NO TAP DANCING ALLOWED

stop putting on a show for everyone
the pseudo positivity
the witty tweet that you stole from someone else
the face tuned Instagram photo
stop

you have nothing to prove to anyone out here.

RACE TO NOWHERE

We're stealing something from the youth
that's not fair to steal and that's
curiosity
excitement about the unknown
a need to explore
a passion to do, to see

instead, in its place we've instilled
an assembly line to "success"
you have to do this, that, then this

and then that's when your life really begins
an assembly line that treats
every child the same
despite their differences

what does this get us?
what does it get them?

when everything in their life has been in preparation for
the big S.U.C.C.E.S.S.
where does that leave the rest of it?
we've put dreams on the backburner
aspirations on the side
forget creativity and originality

it's only about making enough money
until you die
and I get it

I can hear the rebuttals now
money doesn't grow on trees
people have to make a living
people need money to survive
all true, all valid

I ask, what happens when you redefine
success?
success isn't something reserved for the few and far between
only the hard working, only the special

I resent that
I resent that each of us has to prove our worth

that you're a blank piece of paper when you're born
and the only thing that matters is scribbling as many
accomplishments
onto it as you can

I refuse
when you stop racing
when you stop trying to be this or that
when you stop proving yourself
when you accept

accept that there is nothing lacking
nothing you need to prove
when you start living
not because it's what you're supposed to do
but because it what you want to do
what does that look like?

what do you look like?
when you no longer need outward validation
to make your life feel whole

what does it look like when you
define success for yourself?

WHO'S DREAM IS IT?

Is that your dream or someone else's?
how do you know?

there a dreams that don't spring out of organic material
but are manmade, modified, scripted
sliced and diced for decades in labs
ingested by the masses
passed down through generations

goals, promise lands, emerald cities

is that image in your mind your own
or have you seen it before?
was it feed to you?
in so many words, in so many images

and even if it wasn't fed to you
even if you willing picked up the apple
did you know there were other options?
did you see the tree behind the bushes?
or was the apple on the plater, closer, easier, accessible?

there are many dreams that are common
dreams that in similar communities almost everyone has

there's a nation
you might know it
that was built on dreams
most are, but this one was a little different

gold streets, torches to light the way of the downtrodden
dreams that diffused in water like melting ice
and we drank it up

moths to a flame

but whose dream was that?
whose script?

because there were
terms and conditions to those dreams.

that's what happens when you
chase someone else's fantasy

you realize they didn't have you in mind
when they dreamt it.

I'M TIRED OF RUNNING

chase chase chase
that's all anyone seems to do
it's what's expected
there's always something more
work yourself to the bone
heave, stick, pull,

work day in, day out
"come on you don't have time to waste
you've only got one life
and you've got to accomplish aaaaalllllllllll of
thhhhhhhhhhiiiiiisssssss
before you die or before you're 25"
or what's the point?

you've failed
bye bye
you're a nobody
no one knows your name
you don't have riches or notoriety
so that's it
no one will remember you
and all that matters is being remembered
is leaving something behind
that's aaaalll
that's it
that's what everyone wants
to be known, to go down in history
and we're all chasing, chasing, chasing

it's all we want, want, want

and what for? For this?
look around, how's this working out

maybe I don't know anything
but I know what I feel, what I believe
and something doesn't feel right
chasing all day every day
I'm not saying never do anything
but where's the finish line?

Death.

well damn, that's depressing
we all die, but I don't want to run towards it
picking up as many trophies as I can along the way

I want death to be a restful sleep
after a long and eventful day
a day that was so exciting, so fun, so fulfilling
that when you're head hits the pillow you're out

tuckered out by the events, but it's a welcome rest
after knowing you've done something you enjoyed
something worth doing

that's all
that's all I want
I don't want a sleep
where I slump into bed after tirelessly working, stressed, depressed
as an escape

what's it for?
I don't know
I just don't want my life to be a resume

well, she did this, and this, and then that
look at all those gold stars
but did I even enjoy any of it?
is it what I wanted?

Death is inevitable

the only and one constant
in all our lives

one day I won't be in this world
one day I won't wake up
and neither will the people I love

and so when I take my last breath
what will I remember most?
I doubt it will be clocking in and out
I hope it'll be a smile
a laugh
a hug

I hope it will be the moments were
I wasn't working but just being
were life happened
and It didn't have a purpose or a rhyme
I was there I was present

forever captured in my heart
and there's
in yours

that's it.

R.I.P

Sometimes I smile so hard I cry
As if I'm shocked I could smile this hard

So many days without smiles
So many fake smiles
Cracked smiles
Crooked smiles
Broken smiles

But this smile makes my heart ache
Because I mourn for the girl who didn't think she disserved this
kind of joy

And so I smile a little wider
Laugh a little harder

And I shed that tear
Like watering flowers at the grave of a past self

A self that didn't know true smiles
I'll smile for the both of us now
It's ok

We made it.

THE RIVERS I'VE CRIED

I used to think tears were weak
So I drank mine
I chugged so much I almost drowned myself

I wished them away
Wiped them away
Collected them in jars
dumped them in the river

but then I started to realize
that these tears where my demons evaporating

like holy water
I was washing myself clean
Exorcising what haunted me

There are tears that spring from
Visceral emotional blows
Hitting you across the face and leaving a sting

And there are tears that come out of remembrance

They remind us
We're still here
We're still feeling
We're still breathing

Tears aren't weak
They're the only thing we have to clean the slate
The only way to finish and start again

The only thing that reminds us that somethings can't be contained
And placed neatly on the shelf.

SENSITIVE QUEEN

Somedays I wake up laughing
and go to bed crying

and it's like the tide coming in and then retracting
somedays I wonder how it feels to not feel

to not have every day be a kaleidoscope of emotions
to not have every day be tragic and epic
for the pain not to sting a little too long
for the laugh to linger after the joke
for the tears to pour without warning
for the passion to start forest fires.

SIDE EFFECTS

Don't get my hopes up and crush them
Don't

Too many disappointments.
And at least have the decency to apologize
Instead of letting me down and acting like it's my fault

I hate people who try to make
Me feel bad for being hurt

Nope. Not today.

Own up to hurting me
Own up to your part and I'll own up to mine.
You don't get to dismiss my emotions as frivolous?

I spent too many years not trusting how I felt
Because other people told me I was overreacting

It left me empty
In the wrong place every time
Because I didn't listen to my intuition.

NOTE TO SELF

The answers aren't out there
They're not out in the sky or space
They're not in the mouth of someone else

And I know that's difficult
Other's seem to have it figured out
You have all the answers you'll ever need.

ROMANTICIZING ESCAPISM

Sometimes I wonder
what would happen if I just grab some shit and go?

anywhere, drive away, leave everything behind
how far would I get?
Where would I go?

It's easy to ignore the people that care about you when you have
tunnel vision

And I want to drive through that tunnel and end up on the other
side a different person

But do I stay for them or leave for myself.

ROMAN CATHEDRAL

A broken woman with broken words
Trying to write herself back together

Her pen a needle and thread
Maneuvers through the nerves of her skin
To stitch up old wounds never healed
That still ooze

A rag doll on a self
She tries to recreate
To replace
To retrace
Her steps

With this needle and thread
Her sword and holster
Her shotgun and round
Her poison and veil

One woman dies and the other lives
A battle of epic proportion
A cathedral event

Blow the horns
Ready the stallions
Because they've both entered the pit

It's a race
It's a battle
It's a chess match

One spike
One head
Whose will it be?

Clouds roll in, thunder, and the sand dials running low
Times's slipping away through cracks of broken glass
Tick tock, the final hour, the last blow, the shows end
And who won?

The woman writing.

HOW TO LIVE 101

Maybe I missed it?
Missed that moment where everyone else
Learned the basic lessons of how to live

Because this flailing like a fish gasping for life
Is wearing me thin.

A bird with wings
But no sense of direction
No idea where their flock is
Where they're migrating to

I want to believe that I was hibernating
And maybe that's how I missed it
But even bears know what to do when they awake.

UNPLANNED GARDENS

It's easy to be positive when everything's going as you planned

It's easy to smile when you're happy
But when shit hits the fan

Where do you run?

Old habits creep back when you don't know how to cope
Old habits you buried pop up like fresh daises

And now you're watering them with your tears.

PARENTING ADVICE FROM MY INNER CHILD

There are a lot of parents that refuse to see their own flaws and as a consequence they're passing down trauma to their children

This is something no one wants to hear, especially not parents
But I'm going to shed a light on this in the hope that it will help some children have better childhoods

Just because you never could
Doesn't mean your child can't

Just because they don't want to live the life you want for them
Doesn't mean they'll have a bad life

Just because their idea of success if different than yours
Doesn't mean it isn't success

Stop projecting your own insecurities and faults onto your children
They are not your opportunity to rewrite your past
They are not alive to do the things you couldn't

They are here to live. To live. That's it.
Let them make their own mistakes. Their own decisions.

Caging them in doesn't work
And there are many ways to cage a child.
Physically, emotionally, spiritually

This isn't your story to write
None of it

When you make the serious decision to bring a life into this world
have the decency to respect it. You were a child once, as we all were, don't forget so easily.
Stop the cycle of raising your children how your parents raised you.

Do better than they could.

METAMORPHOSIS

New days seldom feel new
You brush your teeth like normal
Same place
Same people

But each day a little
Piece of the puzzle gets added

Each day the big picture
Is a little clearer
And I don't know
What puzzle I'm solving

And sometimes it feels like nothing changes
At all
Day after day
Night after night
But today

I'm the same as yesterday
But not the same as last year

An illusion of
Numbers and dates and calendars
But I can feel the difference
A year makes

I can see the chipped paint
I can feel the tide shift in me

And I know I'm not going to be the same next year
Or the year after that
Or that

Comforting to know

My story is only over
When it's over.

BLACK INK

Writing on the wall
On my face
On my legs

I'm filled with words
That spill out
Pour out
Bleeding out
And

There are words
On my forehead I can't see

And people look at them like they're looking at me
And I see their faces
And I wonder what's written

I try to write on myself
Change my narrative

But the words on me are in permeant
Ink
Ink
Ink
As black as the sky
As black as my hair
As black as the hole I'm trying to fill with words

And I
With a silver pen
And a white paper
Try to write my life
My past, my present

I try to define and redefine the confines

That I see
Written on the walls.

WHAT DO YOU WANT?

What do you want?
I can't answer your questions
I can't tell you what you want to hear.

So you tell me.
Please, because I'm *dying* to know how this ends
Where this goes
How it begins

I know only what I know
Only this moment
Only this breath

So if you want answers
Sorry
All empty
Never had any anyway
So stay and maybe
We discover some together

Whatever
Wherever

It's only a matter of time
The time of right now
Feels divine
And I'm ready for time to stop
And freeze us together

So tell me
What do you want?

DRINK UP BABY

I want to find happiness at end of this bottle
Press full throttle and dive
Into myself
Dip my feet
Into the wet sand that lines my eyes

And discover
Why people
Need me
And need it

What is it about
This
Me
Us
We
That's important, relevant?

At the bottom of the ocean
At the bottom of this wine glass
I'm searching like a deep sea diver looking for treasure

I want the pleasure of discovering
The truth
A truth
My truth
TRUTH

In its purest forms

Some answers
Some ideas
Anything
Anyone
That can fill this

Swimming pool of
Wonder and swarming confusion.

TIP OF THE ICEBERG

The first time I took a drink
I thought
This is it?

This is what Hemingway and Poe and Bukowski
Were chugging down?
This is where they found their comfort?
This is what leaves people empty on the curb?
This what people sneak out of mom and dad's cupboard?
This is what fuels parties
And laughs?

I was underwhelmed
It tasted fowl
Why would anyone subject themselves to that?

How could your happiness be at the bottom of this bottle?
And then I took another sip.

LAZY SORROW

There are days where I don't want to get up
Don't want to talk
Or walk
Don't want to smile
Or say hi
Don't want to pretend

Today my soul is mourning.
What?
I'm not sure

But it's difficult to do anything else
I just want to be still for just a day or two

No noise
No nothing, just silence
No expectations

There are things that people want from me
And I don't know how to give it to them.
I barely know anything at all
And I'm too tired today
To tackle their requests.

ALL THE THINGS I DON'T KNOW

I'm not sure what I'm writing
I sat down
With a pen like I knew what I was doing
And I don't.

But everyone around me looks so good at it
Pretending
And maybe I am too
I can't see myself

I don't have anything
Figured out and it's scary

I want structure
A plan
Control
But I don't have that
and I don't think I should

maybe it's better that way
everyone seemingly knows what they want
who they are
where they're going

What do I know?
All I know is this pen and paper
These questions that I don't have the answer to

That's it that's all.

BLANK

Empty faces
Going empty places
The blank stare out the window
The inspection of the shoes

And who's going where I can't tell
But we're all going

Separate lives
Colliding for one moment in time and I
Might never see your face again
And I'm not sure if I care

I'm just a face
In a sea of faces and so are you
But behind those
Eyes are a life
I can't see

Sometimes I want to peek behind the curtain
That is someone

See all the clockwork and gears
But I'll just stare at blank spaces
With my blank face.

TOO MUCH TO ASK

I need A DAY
One day
Today

Just one
Every once in a while

Just a day
I need
To pause
I need to catch my breath

Like I've run a marathon without training
I'm tired
I'm sore
I'm weak
Unprepared

And I feel the pain seeping into my bones
My soul

So before this snowballs
I'm going to need this
One
1
I.
Day.

SIMPLE

I don't exist
To be likable
I exist because
I am

I AM

It's that simple.

BANG

I don't feel like feeling bad today

So what else you got?
You got criticism?
Comments?
Suggestions?
Shade?

Let's hear it
Let me get my chair

Shoot
Bang
Cause I know this song
Because I already wrote it
So let's hear it

Let's hear the playlist of my life
From your perspective

Please, I'm listening
Who am I?
What's the verdict?

Because you got it
You got me figured out

So indulge me
Whatcha got?

Everything you write I've already written
Everything you say I've already said

So let's hear what grand insight you have about
ME.

Let's hear it.

The stage is yours
Let's take the spotlight off me and put it on you

Cause clearly you've got something I'm missing

Action, play, open curtains.

PRETTY PICTURE

I can't be her
I can't be the girl from the picture

I can't be the illusion
The projection

She's pretty
She's nice
But she's not me
And I'm not her

So what do you want?
Me or a phantom.

YOU THOUGHT

Am I supposed to crumble under your gaze?
Maybe once but not anymore.

DEAR AUTHOR II

Who wrote these rules
You live by?

Was it you?
I hope so.

PRESCHOOL GAMES

I used to look for myself in other people
So I became silly putty
To mold.

Thought they knew better than I did
Because I didn't see my own power.

Thought their opinions were more valuable than my own
Because I couldn't see my own worth.

THE RE-EDUCATION OF ME

Like an open nerve
I felt everything
Every thought, look, snicker
I felt it deep.

I wished it away
Wanted to be unfeeling
Unseeing
Hurt was around every corner
And I didn't have a way to stop it

It took me years to learn that caring wasn't the problem
That my emotions weren't a hindrance
They were tools I could use to navigate

I just didn't know how to use them yet
I had cared about the wrong things
The wrong people.

STUCK

Some people aren't going anywhere, they're stuck.
In the same mindset
In the same pattern.

Some people
Are so realistic they'll never do anything out of the ordinary
And that's ok
There's nothing wrong with average.

But if you want more than the status quo
Or just different
You can't take advice
From stuck people
In stuck places.

BRICKS

Having the words to vocalize your dreams, one brick

Having the watercolors to paint it, two bricks

Having the notes to play it, three bricks

Having the vision to see it, four bricks

That's why it matters where you are. Who you're with. What you're doing. If you don't have the bricks how do you build?

LIVE: FROM THE DRAGONS DEN

I'm entitled to my anger

You don't get to define how I feel
Just because it's more convenient for you

Learn how to take responsibility for your actions
And how you treat people
Instead of everybody else being at fault

And I'll tell you another thing

You can mess up
You can do wrong
I'm tired
I'm annoyed
I'm angry

And it's because of your actions
Now that I'm voicing my anger, you're upset at me.

Fuck you
I will not be silent and be put into a corner because you say so.
If I'm hurt
I'm hurt
There's no overreacting.

Overreacting is a word you use to rob me of my agency

Can you see the steam coming out of my ears?
Can you feel the warmth of the flames?
Don't try to run now, it's too late.

"NICE" "GOOD" GUY

I really llllooovvvee a "good guy"
The I'm a "good guy" type of guy

The *look at me*
I'm nice
Type of "good" guy

The I'm a "good guy"
But…
"good guy"

the let me be passive aggressive
let me make you feel bad about something I did
"good guy"

the I'm the exception
"good guy"

the I'm the victim
"good guy"

and there's nothing more appealing than
a "good/nice" guy who always has to tell you he's a
"good guy".

PRISON BREAK

I'm done with locking up my shame.

Solitary confinement
Stir crossed, deteriotating health, lashing out

I'm tired of my trauma rotting in my stomach

My blood is poisoned
Lead in the water
Carbon dioxide laced in my air

Time to get that detector
That filter
That medicine
That sage
Cross
Salt.

QUESTION MARK

Is my life only worth knowing if I have a list of gold stars?
Is excellence only reserved for the graduates?
       the scholars?
       the I did this and thaters?
Is my existence not worth anything unless it meets standards?

IGNORANCE IS BLISS?

Some pills are too big to swallow.
Somethings I'd rather not think about,
But ignoring it doesn't get me anywhere.

Knowing somethings changes you
And I don't know if it's a good or bad change.

I don't know if this knowledge has
Sparked something
Or killed something inside me

I can't tell yet.

PLAYING WITH FIRE

Does it really matter if I do something bad?
Bad in a way that it only hurts me.
Maybe a little self-destructive
Maybe playing Russian roulette
But no one else gets hurt

So…
How bad is it really?
At least I'm minding my business in my badness
At least I'm not letting it seep onto anyone else

I don't think I'm bad, just desperate
                    just lost and clinging to anything that might
save me.

CAN YOU HEAR ME?

I want all the Gods and Goddesses of the universe to hear me
when I say

I'm trying.

If you guys are all seeing/ knowing, like everyone claims you are,
you know that.

I'm trying, really.
I'm doing my best.
Maybe my best doesn't look like everyone else's but,
I'm here in the flesh
Another day, another breath.

If no one else gives me credit for trying
I hope you'll do.
That's what you guys are for right?
Loving everyone.

So can I get a little?
Just enough to get through the day
And a little for tomorrow too.

Do you want something in return?
I never figured out how this works
Too many missed Sundays or Saturdays I guess.

ROLL THE DICE

Is it all a game of numbers?
How much this, that
Times, add, subtract

How much you got
Count your golden stars

I'm carving tally marks into my skin trying to keep track
I'm ripping out heartstrings keeping them on a rack

Does it matter?
The numbers
Apparently it does
Can't live without em

And when did I sign up for this?
When?
I never asked to play the numbers
But here I am with a pocket full of scratch offs.

MIDDLE OF NOWHERE

Where do I go from here?
And where is here?

Do you see my dilemma?
I'm lost on a blank map.

The world seems to unravel
In my hands
Turns to dust
Concrete substances
Turn to mush
Silly putty and mod podge.

I should be out there
Out beyond the nothingness

But how?

CRY BABY

How many tears do I have to cry before they wash me away in a tidal wave?

MY FIRESIDE CHAT

So, I'm angry.
Angry at a system that values numbers more than people
                    values pieces of paper more than faces
                    values accolades more than how was your
days.
and I'm angry
Angry that living isn't enough
        Being isn't enough.

I've got to do this, that and the other
Time's ticking
Gotta work my life away
But what choice do I have?
What choice do any of us have?

People have to eat
People want homes and things and to be safe
health insurance
All those things cost money.

I guess the price is sacrifice
Sacrificing your time
                    energy
                    soul.

a little melodramatic
I know
But I can't help but look around
                    Look around at people in their 50s
still stressed
still getting by
still yelling
still worrying
about numbers, pieces of paper, accolades

So, I'm angry
Because we all disserve more.

GOOGLE SEARCH: THERAPISTS NEAR ME

I cry so much my tears should have washed me clean by now.
I'm scrubbing and scrubbing
And I'm trying to get this grim off of my soul
And I can't.

It's like it's burned on there
A permeant mark I can't remove.

Is everyone this lost or is it just me?
I'm so lost I can't see up from down
                    left from right
I don't know what's right and wrong.

All I feel is confusion
            delusion.

I want some answers
        some time
        some anything
            anything that can be mine
                    that I can grasp
                    that's real.

I want to rip through my chest and scrape
All the demons out

Scrub the inside of my ribs
And clean away all the hygrographs scratched into my bones,
Light sage in my stomach,
Submerge myself in salt,
Write and write and write,
Until there's nothing on this page but the black ink of my
confessions.

I want to be my own shaman

healer
priest
therapist.

A HYPOCRITES OPINION

I'm tired of pep talk poetry
I want emotion
All and any emotion.

I want to see the confusion
Delusion
Twisting of your inner mind

I want your heart served to me on a platter
I want to peak into your subconscious
Catch a glimmer of your soul.

I don't want advice
I want to see you.

LET IT ALL OUT

Everything I feel turns into tears
Happiness, sadness, anger, frustration.

I used to think it made me weak to cry so much
Until I met someone who never cries.

All that water inside them eroded and wore down all their valleys
Flooded all their fields.

You can tell it was nothing but floods and thunderstorms inside
them
Noah's ark without the ark
And their soul was drowning
They were suffocating themselves from the inside out.

MY CELIE MONOLOGUE

I'm not going to apologize for being alive
I'm not going to lie down for anyone to walk over me
I'm not going to be silent
Not anymore.

I used to be a scared girl
Afraid of her own shadow.

A girl who was sorry for
Everything
For breathing
For thinking

So if I'm talking too loud
Just know I'm speaking extra loud for her.

So if I'm taking up too much space
Just know I'm spreading my wings a little further for her.

So if I'm breathing heavy
Just know I'm taking an extra-long breath for her.

For her
And for me.

I'm here.
Get used to it.

THANK YOU

Maybe I don't know what I'm talking about
But I'm still writing
And you're still reading.

www.ingramcontent.com/pod-product-compliance
Lightning Source LLC
Chambersburg PA
CBHW020548030426
42337CB00013B/1009